COME
TO THE
MOUNTAIN

COME TO THE MOUNTAIN

The Contemporary Experience of Prayer

Stan Parmisano, O.P.

AVE MARIA PRESS   NOTRE DAME, INDIANA 46556

Acknowledgments:

From "East Coker" and "The Dry Salvages," in *Four Quartets,* by T.S. Eliot, copyright © 1943; copyright © 1971 by Esme Valerie Eliot.

From "Morning Has Broken" by Eleanor Farjeon, in *The Children's Bells,* copyright, Oxford University Press.

Scripture texts used in this work are taken from the NEW AMERICAN BIBLE, copyright © 1970, by the Confraternity of Christian Doctrine, Washington, D.C., and are used by permission of the copyright owner. All rights reserved.

International Standard Book Number: 0-87793-337-5

Library of Congress Catalog Card Number: 86-70254

Art, Cover and Text Design by Katherine A. Robinson

Printed and bound in the United States of America.

CONTENTS

EL SHADDAI

Come, let us climb the
LORD's mountain
                              — Isaiah 2:3

It was a pleasant seven or eight miles from the
park where they had left the car to the shelter at
the base of the climb. The path twisted in and up
through cool green forest and over hills of shale
that crunched like glass beneath their heavy boots.
Finally, they arrived in a sun-drenched meadow
still flecked with snow and alive with the sound of
fresh running waters. Sunrise Shelter, it was called
— on account of the small open-faced cabin the
rangers had built there for the convenience of
campers and the occasional climber. But, to his
thinking, it was more like some left-over paradise
or suspended Shangri-la. Only there were the
inevitable mosquitoes, starved in this late spring
for their first blood of the season. Too bad. But a
small price for the sight and sound of all this
primitive wonder and unearthly stillness.

They dropped their packs and sat down on a clump of soft damp grass and, in quiet awe, observed the scene. Behind them gloomed the thick dark forest out of which they had just emerged. On either side of the meadow were steep cliffs of snow and scree topped by patches of stunted pine; and straight ahead angling high into the eastern sky were the last 5000 feet of mountain. It rose gracefully, majestically to its soft rounded crest, all fresh and virgin in new-fallen snow, now purple in the gathering dusk.

He thought about tomorrow's climb. He had tried it once before but had to give it up when he reached the long serpentine spine that linked the rest of the mountain with its summit. His lame leg finally gave out altogether and the others had to carry him back down. Things hadn't gone well for him since, and the connection between his failure here and the rest of his life had often suggested itself. Not that he thought that the one was the cause of the other, but that both emerged out of some subliminal pattern, a kind of symbiotic or synchronistic whole that infested each of his life's fragments. He was almost always tired and depressed, and had several times considered moving away from his present form of life into something new. But after such depth of living, such total consecration, where could he go? All else seemed dull and senseless by comparison, and though he tentatively tried for other loves the original persisted, nagging him into enforced fidelity.

Now after three years he had returned to the mountain, and tomorrow he would try again for the summit. He wasn't quite sure why he was there. Maybe mere superstition, maybe pride. But he did know that something desperately needed to be done, some gesture, at least, had to be made before he gave up altogether. And, strangely, these last few weeks he felt a confidence building in him, a subliminal intimation that this time he might succeed. Succeed here, and then, perhaps, elsewhere. He had his doubts, his fears, but in spite of them or because of them, he felt that this time he just might make it. For one thing he knew better what to do and what not to do. Take it slowly, no need to rush, stop often and rest. He had repeated the phrases over and over like a litany: Play with the mountain, talk to it, don't assault it, take it unawares, make love to it!

At times he had to laugh at himself for talking like a real mountaineer preparing for some spectacular climb. He was no Hilary and this was no Everest. But so much was relative. For him this was as great a challenge as any Alpine or Himalayan peak might be for the professionals. It would take all the energy of his wounded body, lots of stubborn will, and sometimes he would have to say no to reason and common sense. But eventually he just might make it.

Leisurely they set up their modest camp, a few yards in front of the shelter. They gathered some

of the dry wood that lay scattered about and soon
had themselves a bright warm fire with a pot of
thick minestrone cooking above it. As they ate, the
valley gradually filled with shadows and by the
time they had finished their meal darkness had
engulfed all and the heavens were black and
crowded with a million stars. They snuggled close
to the fire, talked for a while, and said their eve-
ning prayer. Then the cold forced them into their
sleeping bags and into the profound silence of the
night.

He would have to sleep well, he told himself,
but he knew he wouldn't. He was too excited, and
the thin cold air only added to his restlessness. He
thought fitfully of the past three years, the waste of
them, his chronic depression still with him. He
recalled, and feebly asked pardon for, that wild
attempt upon his own life and how he had failed
even in that. And he wondered for how much
longer. Would the mountain, after all, be the cure
he longed for, or would it plunge him deeper into
the doubt and darkness? He was hopeful, ner-
vously expectant that here on the mountain. . . .

The long night dragged on. Now and again he
dozed and dreamed crazily, but it wasn't until the
first glimmer of dawn that his mind and body
relaxed and real sleep became possible. It was too
late, the others were already stirring, so he rose
with them. They revived the fire, had their coffee
and bacon and eggs, and then prayed together . . .

Morning has broken
Like the first morning,
Blackbird has spoken
Like the first bird.
Praise for the singing!
Praise for the morning!
Praise for them, springing
Fresh from the Word! . . .

I have raised my eyes to the
mountains,
whence shall come my help. . . .

How different it was to pray here in this vast solitude, so close to a heaven still alive with stars, that
mountain a giant silhouette against an awakening
dawn. *El Shaddai* — the God of the mountain. A
strong and powerful God, a God exalted, to be
feared and worshipped, before whom you knew
you were mere creature — out of nothing and, left
to yourself, tending back into nothing. The God of
the Universe. This God had emptied himself to
become his own creature — the mystery of the
Incarnation. The mountain, then, was a kind of
sacrament. Good. The climb would be a pilgrimage and the summit achieved might yield something of heaven or at least a little less of hell.

They were ready now. The edges of the mountain were glistening from the rising sun behind,
and there was just enough light to see their way by.
It was still freezing cold but they knew that as soon
as the sun appeared the temperature would almost
instantaneously leap to oven-heat. They were silent

as they walked in file up the valley floor. The only
sound was the low gurgle of the stream off to their
right and the crunching of their falling steps on
the packed snow. After an hour of more or less
level ground, the way suddenly and abruptly
steepened, just as the brilliant edge of the sun rose
over the northern spur like a giant's crown, shower-
ing the air with light and warmth.

The other two were younger and athletic, so
he told them to go on while he rested. They could
await him at the spine if they wanted, or go the
distance and he'd join them at the summit. They
thought it over and then moved forward and were
soon out of sight around the first shallow ridges
that darkened the entrance to the tortuous snow
field above. He was alone as he had wanted to be.
Just him and the mountain and the burden of the
sacrifice he bore within. He took off his heavy
jacket and strapped it to his rucksack, and ad-
justed his goggles. Thus prepared against the sun's
heat and glare off the snow he began the ascent.

He took his time, fixing each boot firmly
before raising the other to a step beyond, and
leaning forward, slightly, into his ice axe. He
mounted sideways and always to the left so as to
circumvent the masses of rock and the fissured
snow that scarred the field higher up. Once beyond
these he swung sharply to the right, away from
that mammoth cornice jutting out precariously
over a frightful chasm. Then slowly, painfully,
straight up to the devil's hump — a towering ridge

of volcanic rubble that separated the snow field
from the upper glacier and stole the summit along
with half the sky from his view. Here, at its base, in
its dark, heavy shadow he sat down, breathless and
weary. He looked back over the long, tedious way
he had come in just under three hours — that long
steep sweep of undulating whiteness splashing
against the gray rock and into the green valley far
below. Though the valley was now bathed in light
he could barely make out the meadow at the far
end of it and, of course, nothing at all of the
shelter and camp. Reluctantly he looked up. Yes,
they had named it right. Here was the Satan of the
climb, this dusky heap of ugly loose rock as sharp
as shattered glass. He closed his eyes. It wearied
him just to look at it. Then he discovered he was
thirsty. His sweat began to cool in the deep shade
but his mouth and throat remained parched and
burning. He gulped a handful of snow and drank
from his canteen. Then he took a small flask from
his pack and sipped the brandy. That was good.
Almost immediately it revived him, physically and
mentally. He stroked his leg. It seemed sturdy
enough still. He would continue to favor it. It would
have to be strong along with the rest of him for the
glacier beyond, the spine and that sheer wall of
snow and ice that led directly onto the summit.

He started up. This would be the worst part of
the climb—not the most dangerous, certainly, but
the dullest and most grueling. No firm snow here
to hold his footing, only loose shale that gave way

with every step; two up and one down, and such a
long way to the top. This was where his leg had
begun to fail the last time so he was particularly
careful of it, leaning most of his weight onto the
other. Before he was halfway up his body was
aching, his head throbbing. His depression began
to surface and he was audibly cursing himself for
even having considered that such foolishness
might possibly bring relief. But the hope or illu-
sion of how relatively easy it would be after he had
"overcome the devil" carried him forward. Once he
had crested the ridge he would be able simply to
slide down the short distance to where the glacier
that gently rose toward the summit began.

He was at it over an hour. Sweat drenched his
clothes and his head and heart were pounding as
he rounded the top. But he had made it. The hell
of the journey was over. Yes, the way beyond would
be more difficult, more frightening, but it would
have a beauty and yield a hope that would excite
him more and more as he approached his goal.
Even as he was struggling up the last few yards of
rubble he could feel the cool and tender touch of
the wind blowing across the glacier. When at last
he stood on the narrow crest of the ridge his sweat
dried in an instant and a sudden chill revived him.
Happily, he let go his rucksack and put on his
jacket and scarf, all the while gazing at that soft
white roundness that had reappeared above and
beyond. It seemed so close now but he knew it was
still hours away. He stretched out, full length,

resting his head on his pack. Suddenly he felt nauseated. He turned his head to vomit and retched several times, but nothing came. For an instant he panicked, thinking it was all over. But just as suddenly he felt well again, lighter even and stronger. Thank God, thank God! He would make it now; he was all but certain of it.

As he had anticipated the descent was easy. Like an escalator the yielding scree gently carried him down onto the snow beneath. From there his eyes searched the long stretch of glacier before him. Far up on it he could barely make out two small dots, scarcely moving. That would be his friends. He was both annoyed and consoled. His deep solitary communion with the mountain was broken for the moment, but toward the end he would have companionship when he most needed and wanted it. Soon they would see him too and know that he was all right and still on the move. They'd feel less concerned about "the old man."

As he made his slow, angular way up the glacier he became aware of the unexpected sharpness of its slope and the hardness of the snow compared to that of the field below. It would never, he knew, become all ice — the mountain wasn't high or cold enough for that. Still, in spite of his heavy lugged boots, he would sometimes slip and would frantically and clumsily break his fall with the pick of his axe. The only crevasses were high up and to the left so that if he bore far right he would avoid them. Still, he wasn't sure of the

mountain. The very snow upon which he was
walking might thinly veil a fissure that could
swallow him whole. What a crazy, half-assed way to
climb a mountain, he thought. Again he began to
scruple. All this hazard and risk, and for what? For
something deep within the shadows, lurking,
palpable, but unclear, uncertain. The only sure
thing was this chronic ache in his spirit telling him
it just had to be. Something terribly important
depended on it. As his mind and heart debated the
issue, his body carried him forward.

The wind off the glacier became stronger and
colder as he mounted higher, adding to his worries. It was cool and refreshing at this point but at
the summit it would be a mad freezing gale. In
such a wind could he make it across the spine and
up the wall? But he wouldn't think about this now,
he determined, or anything else that didn't have to
do with the next step forward. He would face the
problem of the wind when he faced the wind, and
not before. Then he felt the pain — slight, but
definitely there in that damn left leg. He stopped
abruptly, heard the panic pounding in his heart,
prayed as he massaged the knee. "Let it hold! I've
come this far. Please, let it hold!" He stood there
like a frozen corpse except for that anxious hand
rubbing his knee.

The pain subsided. He waited unmoving,
expectant of its return. Then slowly he bent the leg
several times, leaning lightly into it. It seemed
sturdy enough, no evidence of dislocation. So he

moved on, tentatively, cautiously. To distract himself he concentrated on those two dots far up the glacier until finally they merged into the black rock of that final ridge.

As he approached the ridge he heard the faint cries of his friends echoing off the rock and down the slope. Breathless, he stopped and weakly raised his arm in recognition, not seeing them yet but knowing that they would soon appear among the huge boulders above. When he did finally see them, about an hour later, he was at the ridge himself and threading his way up through the rock to where they were huddled together and hiding from the lashing wind.

Immediately and with unqualified assurance they informed him that this was where their climb ended. They pointed to the spine and wall beyond. He had seen both before and been frightened by them. Now they seemed even more formidable. From where they watched, the spine appeared razor-edged and the wall massive and absolutely vertical. Again he felt nauseated and depressed and slightly dizzy. The doubts returned. The stupidity, the folly of pitting his limping littleness against this monstrous mountain! Sure, they were right. It would be madness to go on, and gravely immoral. Suicide once again, and this time it would succeed.

Yet he had come all this way, suffered not just the pains of the climb but, he now realized, the doubt and distress of the past years, all toward this moment. It wasn't just a matter of pride. Hell! Topping this relatively tame mountain was nothing he could boast of, to others or to himself. Hundreds had done it before. Nor was it to succeed physically where formerly he had failed. He had failed at countless other athletic ventures with scarcely the slightest desire to return and conquer. This was something vastly different — the message had become less obscure to him with every struggling step of the climb, and now at last the lurking beast within stood revealed. It was something beyond pride and different from ordinary insanity. A kind of mission, maybe, or something involved in mission.

Or perhaps it was a deep and vital prayer that had to be completed, and only in this way! An intimate organic part of the total ritual of his life, and death. However it had begun, this was the way it was ending. He had to reach the summit, or die trying. If pride or sin or insanity lay anywhere it was in the present temptation to turn back and say no to the rest of his life.

He told his companions that he would have to give it a try. So they quietly watched as he stood up and descended the short distance to the spine. As he approached it his hope revived. The edge wasn't as thin as it had appeared above. The wind was severe but if he kept to the leeward side of the ridge where the steep bank of snow was packed tightly against the rock, he would have some protection from it. Tentatively he stepped down onto the snow, wary of the slippery descent to his left. Step by cautious step he picked his way, his ears ringing with the wind's shriek as it blasted through and over the heaped up stone above him. Several times he faltered as the thin line of snow he was treading crumbled, but his hands fixed firmly on that serpentine web of stone kept him safe. As he moved ahead the snow gradually inclined upward merging at the end with the spine's edge forming with it some few square yards of platform at the base of the wall. There he dug his axe into the wall and gripping it against the wind searched the depths on either side. Immediately he realized that if he would slip he must not fall windward. There the mountain's craggy south face plunged sheer and far. On the other side there were at least some 20 yards of sloping snow before it dropped off abruptly, to what depth he could not see. At any rate, supposing a fall, here lay some chance of survival.

Then he looked up — and now he knew he would succeed!   The wall wasn't vertical after all. The pitch of that great cresting cone was mild enough to make the ascent relatively easy and return possible. The wind still thrashed and chilled him but he could stand, though barely, against it. With his axe he cut several steps into the hard snow and more as he mounted higher. Then the wall tapered and rounded inward, and on hands and knees he achieved the summit.

Kneeling there he looked around at that small area of waste and desolation — huge black boulders half buried in the sparkling blue-white virgin snow. Above was the deep blue vault of the sky. To the west a magnificent tremulous red sun was settling down toward the far end of the narrow valley where their camp was pitched. The sun, he quickly calculated, was about three hours from its setting. To the north and south were the sister mountains of the one he had managed. Massively, majestically they towered above the valley floor. He heard their eerie creaking and the sharp crack and crashing of an avalanche somewhere in the distance. So close did their peaks appear in that clean, clear atmosphere that he almost raised his hand to see if he might touch them. All around for hundreds of miles were valleys and mountains, sharply visible all the way to the far horizon. He felt giddy, and wanted to cry. He leaned forward, signed the snow and kissed it, and made his eucharist. "Touched by your hand our world is holy." *El Shaddai*. Having received it from his hands he returned the mountain to God.

He must have been some 10 or 15 minutes in prayer when he became aware that the wind had let up and that he was enveloped by a profound, almost holy silence. The only sounds were the distant creaking and muffled rumblings of the sister mountains, but these only accentuated the stillness within his sacred temple. Reluctantly he stood up and looked to where his companions had been. He could scarcely make them out but he saw that they were waving. He waved back and then watched them disappear into the tall rock and reappear on the snow below, heading back to camp. Then it finally happened. The nausea returned — in his throat, his mouth, and out onto the snow. He hated polluting all that purity and marring the almost mystical experience of the achievement. But even this was part of it, he supposed, and maybe, the best of it. Not only his strength, but his weakness too — so much of that — both were responsible for his being able to offer his prayer on the summit of the mountain, and both accepted by his God. He felt relieved, light and strong. He would make it back all right now. He covered his sickness, took one more look around, and began his descent.

With ice axe as brake, he slid down the wall and landed neatly on the level space below. Since there was no wind to trouble him now he walked securely along the top of the ridge to the rocky heap opposite and down onto the glacier. Then like a wild, happy child he let himself go — running, leaping, sliding, tumbling, using his axe as guide and brake. What had taken him over three hours to climb, he was at the bottom of in a matter of minutes. Again the tedium and drudgery of mounting the devil's hump, but that too seemed short compared to what it had been on the way up. Then swiftly down the opposite side onto the lower field, and more ecstatic glissading and tumbling to

where the snow levelled off and the valley began.
His leg was aching now, but he didn't care. He
could have lost it altogether and he still wouldn't
have cared. That far more severe ache of the spirit
he had suffered for so long — all his life, it had
seemed — was gone and he felt whole. The whole-
ness had nothing at all to do with the integrity of
his physical limbs. He was larger than his body,
larger than that great mountain even. Yet in those
moments of near-ecstasy he enjoyed and was
grateful for his body's strength and power which
had survived, with so few wounds, such a hard and
harsh pilgrimage.

He walked along the valley floor toward the
smoke of the fire he knew his friends had built. It
was deep twilight now, dark shadows everywhere.
He entered the meadow, saw the blazing fire and
the dim silhouette of the shelter behind. His
friends ran to meet him. They cursed him,
laughed, said what a damn fool he had been, but
congratulated him anyway. They had some hot
soup ready for him and steak and potatoes. He
drank the soup and picked at the rest, and tried to
answer their questions about those last nervous
moments at the summit. Then weariness caught
him up; he felt as though he had been drugged. He
removed his boots, felt the sting of blisters and the
ache in his leg. Again, he didn't care. He slipped
into his sleeping bag and almost at once was in
deep sleep. . . .

. . .He was slowly, gently rising through the deep, deep waters. His tired lungs were near to bursting but he wasn't afraid because he could see the light above, filtered through the water and becoming brighter and brighter. Suddenly and violently he emerged. At first there was only a physical feeling of coolness and lightness, then a sense of profound quiet and peace, and finally an awareness of space, infinite space, and he filled it. He was the space. Gradually the peace flowered into joy, not restless or savage, but the tranquil joy of fulfillment. There was nothing more because there was everything. He was poised at the center of it while filling and being filled by the whole of it. He was still himself, most himself, but he was everything else besides. *El Shaddai* and the magnitude of his heaven. . . .

When he woke next morning the sun was already coloring the sky and only a few of the brighter stars remained. His mind was limpid and his body light as the cold crisp air around him. He felt transparent, as though the day was dawning in and through him. He rose at once. This time he lit the fire and boiled the water and, as he began to fry the eggs, woke the others. His body may have seemed all spirit, but his appetite was voracious and he ate his fill. They smothered the fire, cleaned the site, and restored the shelter to its original order. Then, facing eastward, they prayed their last mountain prayer.

26

Mine is the sunlight!
Mine is the morning,
Born of the one light
Eden saw play!
Praise with elation,
Praise every morning,
God's re-creation
Of the new day!

His friends took up their packs and started out.
Without so much as a farewell glance at the mountain he shouldered his own pack and limped
behind them down the long trail back to the park,
and home.

Our lives are a continual parable,
the Mystery of which very few
eyes can see.

from *John Keats*

1

LISTENING FOR GOD

> Whenever you pray, go to your room, close the door, and pray to your Father in private. Then your Father, who sees what no man sees, will repay you.
>
> — Matthew 6:6

One experienced in the ways of God once said, "There's no such thing as prayer; there's only the pray-er." Something to think about. There are as many different kinds and ways of praying as there are individuals who pray. Let's say that prayer is conversation between God and me. What a dialogue that must be! "Deep calls unto deep," says the psalm. God doesn't so much hear my words or read my lips or even try to unravel the tangled skein of my thoughts, images, memories, and desires. He reads my inmost individual heart and anticipates my words and, with me, forms my mind. Together we make the prayer even as the thoughts are shaped and the words spoken. And I can't hear him or even feel him present most of the time. I can only believe, hope that he's there "in the privacy of my inner room" and try to decipher his silent language in the moment of prayer and in subsequent moments of my life.

Yes, praying is a profoundly personal affair. It must

be. God — Father, Son, and Holy Spirit — is most personal, unlike anyone or anything else, fully alive within himself; having his own secrets, his own mystery, yet at the same time opening up to others everything that he is. This is something of what is meant by Father, Son, and Holy Spirit: Each of the divine persons infinitely diverse from the others yet revealing all that he is to them, praying his entire self into them, such that while each remains unique they are absolutely one in the being, knowledge and love of each other.

This wondrously personal God reveals himself to me in much the same way, only my capacity for understanding and love is limited. I can receive only so much of him, as I can take into my lungs only so much of the air around me. There he is, pouring himself out to me, emptying himself for me, as evidenced in Christ born, living and loving, dying and dead and alive again. I open up to him, trying to empty myself that I might receive him as fully as I can. This is my personal prayer, or I should say our personal prayer, his and mine. It is dynamically personal, for it is creative of my person, makes me what I uniquely am. In the beginning the Spirit of God moved over the chaotic waters and out of that "prayer" leapt light and all the world. And the Lord breathed his Spirit into clay and out of that prayer emerged humankind. And each time I truly give myself to prayer, my praying and his, I'm formed anew. I am still I, but with a fullness never before realized.

Where do we go from here? Or have we arrived? Scarcely. Let me put it another way. We fantasize, romanticize about a love in our life, about someone who would know us to the core and whom we would know as deeply. We long to express this inward self that we ourselves scarcely know is there, so we ache for one who holds the key that will unlock the door and let it out.

To all others I might be common, just like everybody else. But to this person, the love of my dreams, I would be one of a kind. She would call me by my name, and for the first time I would recognize it. And I would do the same for her. So it is with God — person to person, deep unto deep, the depth of God unto the depth of God in me. This is prayer, our prayer, prayed only by God and me in the privacy of my inmost heart.

I've suggested that one way of defining prayer is conversation or dialogue with God. But we're closer to the heart of the matter when we say that it is listening for God. I would almost prefer saying it is listening to God except that so often in prayer God is not "heard," and all we can do is continue to strain our mind and heart after him, struggle to be free of the noise that shuts out his voice, plead that he reveal himself and his will to us. In short, most of the time all we can do is expectantly listen for him and patiently await his word to be formed within us.

No, prayer is not so much listening to God; much less is it talking to him. Here we are liable to be more interested in our own words than in his — what we are saying and what we expect to hear. This is where we often go wrong in other areas of communication too. We say, for instance, that one of the chief reasons why marriages fail is a lack of communication. Immediately we think that what spouses must do is to begin to talk to one another, learn to open up, verbalize what they like and dislike about each other and the marriage as a whole. This may be a first step or gesture toward breaking the ice, thawing an oppressive silence, but it's only that.

A second, more fundamental remedy is learning to listen to one another: to let the other talk and to listen to what he or she is saying — really listen to the other and not just to what you are going to say in reply. But this is still not nearly enough. The last and most necessary step of all is to listen beyond the other's words, listen not so much to the words spoken as for those not yet spoken, words buried in the heart of the other which neither knows yet. Here is communication at its best, where it becomes truly creative of the other and of yourself and of the deepening of the relationship between you. It's where communication becomes an act of love.

So it must be with our communication with God, our prayer. Sure, we talk to God. We complain to him, tell him our joys and sorrows, ask his help — like trusting children talking to an understanding mother or father. We also listen to him, to the words he's already revealed to the world at large and those we think he is speaking in our heart. But most of all, and beneath all the rest, we listen for him, for the unexpected word, the surprise message he has for each of us, his wondrous presence in our life which we so often miss because we are looking elsewhere, but rarely looking and listening for him.

2

BEGINNINGS

It took some time and careful searching, but he finally found it. There were other possible routes, but this one, he thought, was the safest and surest for him. He wasn't for danger now. Plenty of that above where the glacier angled high and steep and the summit was a sheer wall of overhanging rock and ice. He walked the thin path that followed the stream to where both left off. Some vestiges of a trail appeared here and there as he picked his way through the mammoth boulders that overshadowed him at every turn, but once beyond these and the cliff that crowned them, all that remained was the broad virgin-white hump of the mountain and his freedom (and fear) to strike out entirely on his own.

Listening for God is not an easy thing. There's so much noise outside us, so much noise and disturbance within. Words, like beasts in a jungle, spring out at us from all directions. Some are interesting, even beautiful, and we strain to hear them over and over again. Others not so interesting, even ugly, yet still they fascinate, or at least save us from that oppressive and threatening silence hovering within. And so we turn the TV or the radio or the stereo on or we dial a number or we talk or sing to ourselves. If all this fails to check the ever emerging silence, then in panic we may even begin to talk to God or scream at him, pleading for help. So a million million words build into a thick high wall shutting out all sight and sound of God as he is in himself and is always whispering (not talking) to us.

So there are invitations and methods developed through the ages for listening for God — invitations to accept the silence and methods for breaking down the wall and leaving ourselves naked, empty, exposed and poised for God's word alone. True, these methods, which are shared by many, are not of themselves prayer. As I've said, prayer is most personal: God speaking to me out of the intimacy of his deeply personal life to the intimate recesses of mine. No two pray-ers are alike, no two prayers alike if the praying is genuine. Each time a true lover says "I love you" it's different than any other lover has said it, and different than any other time he himself has said it. Always a newness and freshness in living prayer. But though the praying may be different in every single case the ways of getting into prayer may be common to many. The field from which we commence our flight we often share with others, but once off the ground we fly our separate ways.

Many of these methods are old and consecrated. They've evolved out of an understanding of the human psyche, its virtues and vices, and out of the practice of holy people. Some methods are helpful for some, but not for others. There are Buddhist and Hindu and Moslem ways of praying, and hundreds of ways within these, and countless methods within Christianity. Within Catholic Christianity alone I think of Benedictine, Carthusian, Franciscan, Dominican, Carmelite, Jesuit methodologies and all their various offspring. I think of the silent prayer of the contemplative and the speaking in tongues of the charismatic. So many fields from which to choose. God's great plenty!

Before choosing one or other of these methodologies

two admonishments should be heeded. First, the temptation is to flit from one of the many offerings to another without giving any one of them a chance to help us get off the ground into true and personal prayer. We end up making an end of what is only a means. Thus we should choose one method and stick to it, altering it, perhaps, according to present need, but persevering in it until it's obvious it is no longer for us.

Secondly, each of these methods is rooted in a culture or some aspect of a culture, and many of them are inseparable from the religion out of which they originally arose. Here the temptation is to try to divorce the method from the culture or the religion, to use it simply as a trick or exercise which then lulls us into thinking we are grounded in prayer. In truth to profit from Eastern ways of meditating we've got at least in some way to be rooted in Eastern ways of living. To grow in the spiritual exercises of St. Ignatius we've got to be part of the life dear to Ignatius. To pray the simple "Jesus Prayer" efficaciously we've got to know and love Jesus and strive to keep his word.

Thus the second admonition: We should choose a method in harmony with our total personality. With this as our center we may then safely borrow from techniques and practices foreign to us but which we conceive to be helpful in developing our fundamental orientation.

If we observe these two precautions we can take these beginnings and use them toward prayer proper. Then they may become good and solid ground from which we can take flight and to which we can return for further bearings and direction. And if we remember that a good beginning is halfway to the end we'll take proper care to develop within ourselves some fitting, personally compatible methodology so that God's silent word begins to be born within us and our whole being becomes attuned to listening for and to it.

3
THE DARK AND THE LIGHT

I think of the Magi setting out from home and country, moving across vast stretches of desert, braving the heat and the cold, falling prey to thieves and robbers, maybe, looking up (or within) for the sign and sometimes finding it, mostly not, and always wondering about the end of the journey, what they would find there and not find.

And I think of them arriving, after the disappointment at the palace, and now at the greater disappointment of this: a smelly manger, a mere girl of a mother, a shy withdrawn peasant who looked to be the father, and this little bundle of almost nothing. All for this! And yet . . . and yet they should have known, these men of wisdom, from the beginning. The truth sought isn't always the truth given. In the end it's just about all his doing. Only the surprise is ours.

Contemplation is one of the oldest, most consecrated ways of praying, one which, when perfected, runs like a thread through all the others. It's found in various forms under a variety of names in both Eastern and Western traditions of prayer. In our time and place it has been resurrected in still other forms and under other names, such as centering prayer, desert prayer, Arica, Transcendental Meditation, the prayer of stillness or quiet, of emptying, surrender, abandonment. Not all of these are of equal intensity or value. In fact, many of the modern methods are quick, easy, watered-down versions of the great contemplative prayer of Christian tradition, mere beginnings, often faulty beginnings of the original fullness. But the sun is revealed even over muddy waters, and some beginning, I should think, is better than none. So let us begin . . .

I first find myself a quiet room, chapel, church, or nook of nature — someplace where the noise outside is minimal, where the silence is deep and, if possible, "holy." I kneel or sit or stand, comfortably, but not too comfortably (I want to pray, not sleep!). I close my eyes as a further gesture of shutting out the world and concentrating on what is within. I relax my body, trying to free it from all those tight, heavy cords of tension that bind me to my everyday world. I breathe slowly, deeply, to help break those tensions that bind me to my inner chaos. Liberation is the word, freedom from my body and the body of the world.

Now the more difficult work begins — the freeing, the emptying of my spirit. My mind, memory, and imagination are filled to overflowing, cluttered with thoughts and images. I let them all go, even holy thoughts of God, Christ, the Saints. They may be good and salutary, but not now. Now, in this time-out-of-time of contemplative prayer, there must be only darkness. Sure, the images and thoughts will return almost as soon as they're banished, but they must again and again be expelled or ignored.

Sometimes it helps to hold one strong image or word like God, Jesus, Life, Death. Centering on it I lose the others, but as soon as possible I surrender it too, and try to remain in the purity of the dark. Next I empty my will

of all desires and feelings. No hatred or bitterness, no re-
grets over the past or worries about the future, no longing
for life or death, no love, not even for God; no faith even,
not now. For now I surrender it all to him, though even
this I don't think about now. I let it all go in a gesture of
complete and total abandonment, confident that when
my prayer is finished all that is good in what I've laid
down will be returned to me better still, and all that was
crooked will be made straight. But even this I don't think
about now . . .

> I said to my soul, be still, and wait without
> hope
> For hope would be hope for the wrong
> thing; wait without love,
>
> For love would be love of the wrong thing;
> there is yet faith
> But the faith and the love and the hope are
> all in the waiting.
>
> Wait without thought, for you are not yet
> ready for thought:
> So the darkness shall be the light, and the
> stillness the dancing.
> (T. S. Eliot: *East Coker*)

If all there was to contemplative prayer was this
emptying of self — the method — it would almost be
enough. In fact, many of the modern adaptations and
variations of it and forms of Eastern meditation end here.
They regard this total surrender of self and world, this still
and quiet abiding in darkness, the consummation not only
of prayer but of life itself. One experienced in contemplative prayer can see why. For within this surrender and
darkness we gain a freedom — freedom from world and
self, a new-found independence from the pull and weight
of things. Our idols are smashed. All those limited and

limiting images and ideas we've had of God fall away and
we begin to grow in a new faith and love and hope that
moves beyond image and idea into Mystery — the "mysterium tremendum" of God. And we become ripe for that
peculiarly Christian love called *caritas*—a love that looks
to the other not for one's own but for the other's good,
which is precisely the orientation contemplative prayer
strives to achieve.

In the Christian tradition of contemplative prayer
this is only a beginning, good and necessary, but far from
the perfect thing prayer is meant to be. John Tauler, the
14th-century Dominican mystic, said: "As often as you go
out of yourself with all that is yours so does God come
into you with all that is his." Here is where the method
ends and that private, personal dialogue between God
and the individual begins. Not that the two are really sep-
arable. All through the effort to be clean of self and filled
with God, God is speaking and his word is being formed
within us. It's not a matter of before and after but of here
and now. The very moment I surrender myself God is
there where *I* had been. This is what Tauler is saying. But
there comes a point when denial is transformed into affir-
mation, emptiness into fullness, and darkness to light. In
the innocence and freshness of spiritual childhood we hear
and speak with our Father/Mother God. Having with
God's help entered into the dark and suffered it to come
upon us, we now find him carrying us through the dark
and beyond ourselves to wherever and whatever he wills.
Prayer sought ends in prayer given. Our job now is simply
patience, a humble abiding in his lightsome presence, a
quiet listening, not for him now but to him, for he speaks
and his servant hears.

In *The Ascent of Mount Carmel*, St. John of the
Cross admirably describes the process in the poem that

begins his detailed account of the soul's odyssey to God.
The beginning is darkness, stillness of mind and heart,
only the intense desire to venture forth and the first unob-
served steps.

> In a dark night
> With anxious heart enflamed
> Forth unobserved I went
> My house being now at rest.

But in the end the self-abandonment and self-forgetting
are seen to terminate in something, Some One, richly pos-
itive and tenderly loving, and all is in his hands:

> I abandoned and forgot myself,
> Laying my face on my Beloved;
> All things ceased; I went out of myself,
> Leaving my cares
> Forgotten among the lilies.

As a first step, then, we enter into the dark. But we
are not to become enamored of it. For our goal is not
darkness but light; it is not to be empty but filled; it is not
to be nothing, but in my resurrected self to love and be
loved by him who is everything; not to be free of the
world, but to be free for God. That darkness, which
through a long and difficult process we have created and
suffered to be created within us, turns out to be simply
the rendezvous for love. "So the darkness shall be the
light, and the stillness the dancing," adds Eliot who would
have us wait without love, faith, and hope.

The Christian contemplative, therefore, is one who
at best has learned to love — to hear and be heard by the
heart of the beloved. But the love, although always expected and longed for, must not be rushed. Not in my
time, for I am no longer there, but God's time. He may
indeed be there throughout and I unaware. "Truly," cried
Jacob as he awoke from that marvelous dream of his in

the wilderness, "the LORD is in this spot, although I did not know it" (Gn 28:16). But always we must remain pure of our ideas and expectations of love, and patiently await the unexpected visitation.

4

A NEW LANGUAGE

Be brave and persevering, said the King, and
you shall surely have your reward. Providing,
of course, you entertain no expectation of receiving it.

To be still and silent before an unknown God, to forget my every idea and image of him and of all else, to remain in darkness — in short, to begin to pray contemplatively, is no easy matter. Few attempt it, and of those who
do, few persevere. How do I empty myself when I'm full
to the brim and overflowing with myself and the world?
How disrobe myself of idea and image and desire when
these are my lifeblood, as native to me as the mind and
heart that give them birth? As I begin my prayer, no
sooner do I let one image go than another takes its place. I
free myself of one desire and another emerges or the same
one returns almost at once, more tenacious and disturbing
than before. And I find myself ridiculously observing myself at prayer, critiquing my progress or lack of it.

But what am I to expect? Nothing really worthwhile
comes easy. It takes time, ingenuity, perseverance, and often outside help. It's like learning a new language. You've
got to buy the books, maybe get a teacher, sweat through
the grammar, build your vocabulary, spend hours listen-

ing to, reading and speaking the language, and suffering
the embarrassment of a million mistakes. If you're at all
serious about the language you'll go off and live for a time
among its native speakers. And once you have it down pat
you've got to use it continually or it will be easily lost.
Well, prayer is a new language, the unspoken, unspeakable language of God. He once became flesh and spent
years learning our language. With him as our master
teacher, we must take the time and means and exert the
effort to learn his. And just as he, surely, stumbled and
stammered at the start trying to learn and shape his human words, so we may expect him to be understanding
and gracious with us in our most faltering efforts toward
contemplative prayer.

We are not to look for success here, for reasons which
should be obvious by now. First, because we've really no
measure by which we can gauge it. True, we aim for
darkness, and so darkness achieved would appear to be
success; unachieved, failure. But that darkness is the Light
of God which may well be there beneath any lingering
and troubling idea, image, or desire. After all, our part in
contemplative prayer, though important, is the lesser part.
We make the gesture, surrender all as best we can. The
rest is God's work which is deep, intimate, and secret, often hidden even from ourselves.

Another reason why we're not to look for success in
this prayer is that its whole point is to take our minds off
ourselves and fix them solely upon God. My success as
well as my failure, my virtues as well as vices, my life as
well as death — all, absolutely all is now in his hands. In
this my contemplative prayer my attitude must be that of
St. Catherine of Siena: "I am the one who is not; he is the
one who is."

It can readily be seen, then, how contemplative

prayer must steadily be worked at before we become at all proficient. Like learning a new language, like creating a work of art, it takes years in the making. Years, first of all, of trying to live a life open to God at every turn. Prayer must not be thought of simply as a mental exercise, a cerebral gymnastic whereby I achieve a peaceful nirvana or bodily or spiritual energy. I must open up my mind and the whole of my life to God in darkness, both mind and life continually moving out of myself into him, whatever the peace or energy or lack of it may result. Many cannot pray because their life is too agitated or disturbed, off-center. How to remain still and quiet before the Lord while storms rage within? How to begin to calm the storms and heal the havoc except by rising above them in prayer to where he is "who cannot change and who is never shadowed over" (Jas 1:17)? Prayer and living, contemplation and morality — they are organically one and are meant to grow together. But this takes time and effort, what the holy understand as persevering asceticism of body, mind, and spirit.

Further, contemplative prayer takes years of daily practice of disciplining mind, body, and spirit to "sit still" and suffer the darkness to grow. So we must give considerable time each day to it. We don't just dip into the pool and pull out and figure we're the better swimmer for it. We've got to linger awhile, move around, taste the water and feel the cold and, yes, overcome the fear before we and the waters begin to feel at home with each other. The same is true in music or art or science. There's always the warm-up time, time for washing away the old and getting into the new, time to exercise and exorcise the whole of us so that, made pure and flexible, we can move into our painting or music or thought, understand it, be absorbed by it, become one with it. It's no different with prayer.

Once we become proficient at our contemplative prayer the warm-up time diminishes until it's vanished altogether. As soon as we will to pray, all is forgotten, we are emptied of self, and that deeply personal dialogue with God begins. Now we can pray anywhere, anytime — for an instant, an hour — and without any visible preparation. We can converse with others, go about our work or play, but always our contemplative prayer remains intact. It's at this level that St. Ignatius of Loyola's observation rings true: it's not the quantity but the quality of prayer that counts. But, until this moment is reached (and afterward!) quantity does count for something, and we must give prayer space and time of its own.

We are not to watch the clock and count the minutes or hours which we spend at prayer. Rather we should surrender ourselves to that deeper time within us that measures movement, not our movement, but God's eternal stillness. Again, we let everything go including time and the worry about time. We simply rest in his present moment and let him release us when he wills.

But always we're concerned about ourselves, aren't we? Am I doing right or wrong? Am I loved or unloved? What shall I do with my life? Hardly ever do we escape ourselves. "God's deep decree bitter would have me taste. My taste was me," as Gerard Manley Hopkins laments. And so with my contemplative prayer the *whole* purpose of which is to move me out of myself and into God alone, I find myself asking: What is happening to me in and through it? What am I getting out of it? Or is it simply a waste? Don't ask such questions, or if they are already there, ignore them. Else you're back with yourself and away from God.

Something does happen to you during this prayer. It must. Again, as the mystic Tauler declared, you cannot go out of yourself for love of God without his coming into you in equal measure. Where you once were God now appears and functions. Those images, ideas, and desires which seemed so much a part of you now become the images, ideas, and desires of God. Your very heart, as St. Catherine of Siena experienced, is exchanged for his. You are left, not as a void or vacuum, but with another, fuller life. You begin, however slightly at first, to see with God's vision, love with his love, act with his power and sureness, suffer his pain. You may not see or hear or feel God as you pray. No visions or locutions. So much the better, for these are relatively unimportant and, as the holy ones in all the great religions insist, are more to be shunned than desired.

You will, however, begin to see and hear God afterward, by a kind of indirection, like the reflections of the sun on still or stirring waters, on plant and animal and humankind, or like the unspoken meaning between the lines of a good poem. All of creation begins to split and crack and open up to you revealing God at its heart, God who is its heart as well as yours. "Deep calls unto deep" — the God within you to the same God within everything and everyone else. Still, don't look even for this. If you're faithful to your prayer, it will happen, but don't look for it. Simply let it happen when it does. In the meantime continue to be still and alert in God's light which is, for now, your darkness. And then trust that though many other things that you do may be waste, here, in your contemplative prayer, at least some of your day, some of your life, has been saved from perdition.

Yes, what I try to do in this prayer is what I long to do in everything: forget myself in the remembrance of the other. *Caritas* — loving another not for mine but for the other's sake. But can I really forget myself and become absorbed in the life of another? Sure I can. See the loving mother totally unself-conscious as she contemplates her baby at her breast or at play or taking those first uncertain tentative steps. See Teresa of Calcutta holding a starving child, staring into those huge dull eyes, absorbed in them, and saying: "She will live. There's God's life there." See one deeply immersed in prayer or music — ecstatic, *ek-stasis*, standing apart from self, out of time and place and self in something, someone beyond.

> Music heard so deeply
> That it is not heard at all,
>   but you are the music
> While the music lasts.
>   (T.S. Eliot: *The Dry Salvages*)

I have had moments, flashes of it, and know it to be the stuff of heaven, what I'm meant for ultimately. But always the return to the taste and weight of me, to self-consciousness, self-interest, often at the expense of others. But at least in this my contemplative prayer I try and try again to forget myself and remember only God. Among other things, it is a beginning exercise in the love that looks only to the other.

5

IMAGELESS PRAYER AND JESUS

"I am the sheepgate," says Jesus. But a gate,
any gate, is to pass through, not remain under.

Some devout and knowledgeable Christians harbor a
suspicion about the kind of contemplative prayer we've
been considering. They feel it is not Christian, and for
two good reasons. First, it's not grounded in Christ, has
nothing to do with the life of Christ, is even reluctant to
mention his sacred name. Indeed, it would empty self
even of the thought of and desire for Christ, as of every
other thought and desire. Secondly, it is a deliberate,
planned bodiless prayer in seeming manichaean violation
of Christian reverence for the totality of the human person
and for the visible material universe as the visible, tangible sacrament of the invisible God. In this life, at any
rate, we are to know and love God not directly or in an
imageless void or a "cloud of unknowing" but in and
through word, image, idea, especially the quite visible incarnate Word who is his Son.

These objections or reservations are well taken and
ought to be pondered by every Christian seriously engaged

in prayer. This holds true especially in our time when Christian forms and methodologies of prayer are being so strongly challenged and influenced by those from the East. In Eastern meditation, except where it has been influenced by Christianity, the ideal is almost always non-incarnational. It is a stark divorcement and detachment, in prayer as in the rest of life, from all that is visible, material, and of the flesh — a detachment, moreover, that must be complete and final.

But the objections can be resolved. First, it is true that for the Christian, prayer, as all of life,must be Christ-centered. But Christ is God as well as man, and we are to come to the divine through the human — the unseen, unthought, unspeakable divine. Christ is my way, my truth, and my life—the quiet human, visible Christ, but also Christ in depth, which is the transcendent godhead. Thus Christ himself while offering himself as the way, truth, and life continually pointed beyond and within himself to the Father:

When you pray, say "Our Father. . ."

The Father is greater than I. . . .

Father, into your hands I commend my spirit.

One of the hazards of Christianity is to diminish God, to remain in the lowliness which he descended to, forgetting that the main reason he became human was to exalt us, to tap the graced potentiality of flesh and matter to become his own divine, eternal life. Christ spent years struggling to learn our human language but only that he might better teach us to expend the time and energy to learn his language, which is one of dynamic awe-filled silence, of creative, contemplative love.

Secondly, contemplative prayer, though basic to all my praying, is not the only kind of prayer I must pray.

Other kinds of prayer and ways of praying, some of them quite verbal, imaginative, and cerebral, help form the totality of my prayer life. All must unite, must feed on one another, if my overall prayer is to be truly Christian.

I must, for instance, come to my contemplative prayer out of past and present meditation upon the life of Christ. I must hear and read the scriptures, especially the gospels, and the words of holy, learned people opening up the scriptures to me. I must prayerfully think of Christ in terms of my life in my world, and of my life in terms of his, and try to act accordingly. In fact, it's what I've learned over the years about Jesus that inspires me to be poor in spirit, to leave all and follow him — follow him not just as he moves compassionately among people but as he continually draws apart alone into the desert to pray to and with his Father.

So filled am I with a lifetime of hearing and thinking of Christ and his life that he, in visible humanity, spontaneously arises before me even as I try to empty myself and be as nothing before God. And when distracting ideas and images and desires intrude I find the simple words that keep bringing me back to emptiness and darkness are *Jesus, Mary, God, Father* — all taught me by my Lord Jesus in and through his church.

It's Christ himself, both human and divine, who holds me to my purpose even as, I trust, it is he who directs and purifies it. Finally, it's because I've been able in this prayer to rise with Christ above the world that I can now see more in it, the best in it, and help raise it beyond itself into him who makes "all things new."

6

PRAYER AND THE OTHER SIDE OF DYING

"I wish I was dead," he grumbled. "Do you now?" she replied, and smiled. He smiled too as he realized the absurdity of the words. No one can wish for death; only for another kind of life if only one of continual, peaceful slumber. We're caught up in life, trapped by it. Perhaps because we're caught up in God, trapped by him, however free we may seem to be of him. He's got to live, since he is life. So do we, having his very life breathed into us. It's simply a question of the kind or level of life, and there are so many levels, circling, broadening, deepening. The tragic entrapment is to drift only in a single orbit till life falters and splutters and gradually, though never fully, fails.

My contemplative prayer, in which I try to forget all, let everything go and remain naked and alone before an imageless God, teaches me about death and prepares me for it. All genuine prayer is a dying, even the simple, common prayer of petition. To those who asked for a comfortable, prestigious place in his kingdom, Jesus' spontaneous reply was: "You do not know what you are asking. Can

you drink the cup I shall drink or be baptized in the same
bath of pain as I?" (Mk 10:38)

It is dangerous to ask God for anything, for in his
generosity he gives more, gives the best, and it seems the
best is somehow bound up with death:

> "Unless the grain of wheat falls to the earth
>   and dies,
> it remains just a grain of wheat.
> But if it dies
> it produces much fruit" (Jn 12:24).

Much more than the prayer of petition, my contemplative prayer has to do with death. Maybe that's why it's
so difficult to pray it. Something in me refuses to let go. I
cling tenaciously to the life I know, the images and ideas
and the thousands of desires that bind my will to time and
space. I think I'm letting go and surrendering all I am,
that he might be all in all. In that time of prayer I may
even fancy that like St. Paul I want to die and be dissolved
in Christ, and that I'm quite up to doing so. But at bottom neither I nor God is deceived.

I remember how at one time in my life I thought myself altogether fearless about death and was even longing
that it come, and come quickly. Not that I was sad or depressed, much less suicidal. I simply wanted another kind
or level of life I had sometimes glimpsed in precious moments. Then one day I was off on a climb, alone and with
none of the necessary gear, which I wouldn't have known
how to use anyway. The cliff was tall and almost vertical,
beyond my strength and skill. But in my carelessness I
thought I'd give it a try. Three quarters of the way up my
heart began to pound, not from exertion but fear! Without my noticing it the rock had become completely vertical and seemed now ominously to arch over me. I had to
give up and return. But there was no return! Only some

30 yards of sheer drop to the hard rubble below. My infant fear grew to panic. I froze to the spot and even began to whimper. I prayed, desperately, cowardly, superstitiously, thinking of the life, the physical life I did not now want to lose!

Finally I calmed myself enough to make my choice, the only possible one, really, and began inching my way toward the summit. I reached it, and still don't know how. I lay stretched along the broad top of the cliff which, on the opposite side, gently and safely sloped down into the valley below. I was laughing now, crazily, for joy in the life I thought I had surrendered to God repeatedly in my contemplative prayer.

I'm more modest now when I pray. I still make the gesture and want it to be true, but I've long since learned that there's more to dying than simply wanting to. There's that in me that clings and cleaves even though I think I'm free of it. But that's all right, that's good, the way it should be. My primal instincts implanted in me by God himself, tell me so, but so also does my contemplative prayer, less immature now than in my younger years. For this prayer is not just the darkness, the nothingness or death in which I try to suspend myself, but it is the light and life of God, which becomes also my light and life. Death is only one part dark and nine parts God and me resurrected in him. I make the gesture of laying down my life, surrendering all, but all the while I know that the best of what I am he holds and, in the very instant of surrender, gives back to me blessed and purified and holding me fast. I try to let go of life, but God's life, now mine, will not let go of me. Such is my prayer and such, I hope, will be my final dying.

7

PRAYER OF REMEMBRANCE

It was one of those crazy moments outside of
time. I was lying abed in early morning,
thinking of nothing and of everything, when
the memories came flooding in — slowly at
first, then altogether, tumbling over each
other, blending with each other, till all my
life was there in one vast ocean of vision. And
it all added up to this present moment of me
lying there, me as I was and was to be. And
even the dark, forbidden corners were bathed
in light, and the dead were dancing.

Strange how prejudices, distortions of attitude and
thinking, can take hold. How subtly they grow and insidi-
ously destroy, and all the while I think I'm being true. I
think my faith, my theology is sure and complete, but little by little it's been closing me off from God and his
world rather than opening me up to them.

I have a philosophy of life which has been years in
the making, but without my noticing it life itself has
passed it by. It might have been good enough for the old
world but it says little if anything about the new. I've gone
out to others in love and concern, but gradually, beneath
my consciousness, my love has been cooling and souring as
I've begun to see them as they truly are — limited, falli-

ble, treacherous, mean — so unlike my idealized con-
structed idea of them. I scarcely realize what's happening.
So tricky the mind and heart, always slipping, sliding,
and always falling short of the real. And so in my contemplative prayer I try to empty myself, forget all I have ever
known, believed in, cherished. I try to surrender it all into
God's hands. What's false he discards, what's good he returns, altered, perhaps, but real, true, current, alive.

In the presence of God, having forgotten all, I can
begin to remember, not fantasies and fictions of past and
present, but what actually was and is. For now it is not so
much my remembering as God's within me — that pene-
trating depth and breadth of vision that sees into the heart
of things. And more than this: I will remember not as a
matter of mere nostalgia in which I sentimentally dwell
upon things past or almost past. Rather, I will remember
expansively and creatively, for beneath my own memory
the large and creative memory of God is at work. Placing
others in God's memory, which is now the depth of my
own, I see them in a more diffusive, generous light. I
think of them as having been, in God's providence, for
me, and for what's deepest and most precious in me, my
"pilgrim soul." Here even my so-called enemies are seen to
have had creative purpose, having, however unconsciously
and indirectly, helped shape my life toward God.

The same may be said for my sins: though they were
as scarlet, they now appear white as new-fallen snow. But
those whom I now remember I also see simply as themselves, known and loved by God, alone and unique in his
presence, whatever they may also have been for me. *Caritas!* This is one of the reasons why the Christian religion
would have us pray for individual people and things and
not simply leave everything to the will of God. In Christian belief God is concerned not just for the general wel-

fare of the world but for each and every person and thing and movement within it. So we must affirm this belief in our prayer by looking at and appreciating the details of the world and focusing on the individual; in short, by becoming big enough to enter into God's very particularized providence.

I recall, then, and pray for my friend or enemy, my vocation or job, rain or sunshine as needed, the good health of my family or my dog or cat, a new love or an old one — things of consequence and apparently inconsequential things. Placing all of this singly in the hands of God, in his memory, reminds me that each and every particle of it is his, has his touch upon it and purpose within it, and so is deserving of my love, reverence, care, and gratitude.

Because of this new, expanded awareness born of such prayer I become truly creative of those whom I remember. It's pretty much our attitude of mind and heart that makes or breaks nature, including human nature, for it is attitude that shapes the act, that in fact creates or destroys. If, then, I regard others as referable not just to me but to something much larger, and if I consciously understand that they are held and loved by God, then I will at least be slow to get in the way of their growth, and at best I will help them grow.

If the dogs and cats and fishes of the sea, the earth, the rivers, trees, and lakes are not just for me but, in God's providence, I am also for them that they might flourish better, then I shall foster rather than diminish them. If I pray for the continuance of my job or vocation I shall become aware of its universal importance, realizing that it's not just for me — for my wealth or power or comfort or prestige — but I am for it, obliged by God and the needs of others to use it honestly and creatively. If I pray for a certain love, again I learn that that love isn't just for me but I am for it. So I try to nourish it, reverence it, and suffer and encourage it to grow beyond me.

At this point, and for this reason, the prayer of remembrance becomes contemplative and sometimes returns altogether to its prayer of origin, that of total forgetting. Continually placing all in God's hands, in his memory, draws my attention more and more to his presence, and so sometimes I forget the thing I'm praying for and am absorbed solely in him. This is the very process we find at work in the prayer of the church. In all the prayers within and surrounding the Eucharist we pray for individual, particular things and concerns, but each of the prayers ends with praise of the great triune God: "This we ask through our Lord Jesus Christ, your Son, who lives and reigns with you and the Holy Spirit, one God, for ever and ever." In the prayerful remembrance of the details of his creation we find the Creator himself, and we rest in him.

There is still another way in which we become creative of others in this prayer of remembrance. When we pray for others, when we remember them before the Lord, we think of ourselves as asking God to help them. The image is of a triangle. From them across to us, needing our prayer; we up to God, asking on their behalf; and finally God and his benefits down to them. The image is true, but it is not complete, for there is also a kind of horizontal giving and receiving. In our prayer for others we ourselves directly touch and raise them up. Here is where such seeming non-physical activity as telepathy and psychokinesis finds centuries of Christian substantiation. As St. Paul tells us, we are all one mystical or spiritual Body with Christ. We interact with one another not just physically in and through our senses but spiritually by the

movements, gifts, talents, prayers of our spirit, which con-
stitute a unique non-physical energy that pervades the
universe. This is why Jesus condemned not just evil
actions but also evil thoughts: not simply because they
pollute one's own action which then works toward the de-
struction of others, but simply as thoughts, if unopposed,
they can negatively affect the world.

It's the same, then, for good, creative thinking and
loving. Even though I don't visibly express it, even though
I can love only at a distance and in secret, my love pene-
trates others and helps transform their lives and raise
them to God. In other words, in and through my prayerful remembrance of others both God and I are creatively
present to them.

The method of the prayer of remembrance is simple
enough. We come to it from our contemplative prayer of
forgetting. Having given all into the memory of God we
begin gently to reclaim it, or rather suffer it to re-emerge
in our purified memory. We think back over the years or
forward from our beginnings. We recall mother, father,
sisters, brothers, aunts and uncles and cousins, friends and
enemies, teachers, ministers, doctors, simple acquaint-
ances. Each of them individually, as God himself thinks of
them. The litany, of course, grows longer as we grow
older. But there's no rush to get through it. Sometimes the
inclination is to dwell on a single person. Then follow it,
then gently let him or her go for some other, always placing each in the loving care of the Lord. It's remarkable
how seemingly lost memories return — people, places,
things, all still so much a part of us and we of them. We
feel our lives expanding, and we no longer feel helpless
with regard to a past we thought was gone or a present
beyond our visible sphere of action. And no, we need not
worry that we can't in a single sitting get through the

whole of our litany. There will be other times for such prayer, and in the meantime we know that the un-named ones are in God's long, deep memory which our contemplative prayer has made one with our own.

8

PRAYER OF ALL CREATION

"I have the strangest feeling," he said, "that all of this has happened to me before in some other life."

"Quite possibly it has," she ventured. "And do you think, perhaps, that life might have been God's?"

Part of the prayer of remembrance, and an exercise in it, is what I call "the prayer of all creation." Here again, the first movement is to forget, to empty myself of every creature and shadow thereof.

Once I've done this as best I can, I let my cleansed and expanded mind and heart reach out to the universe, piece by piece. In a quiet wood within sound and feel of the great Pacific, I close my eyes and in spirit travel the length and breadth of my native state, wanting to touch lovingly every individual within it, loving its mountains and rivers and lakes and all its teaming life whether under ground, under water, wandering in hills and valleys or flying in the air or walking its city streets.

I move across the Pacific, my spirit touching each of the islands and all who inhabit them. Across Asia and Africa and Europe, across the Atlantic to the States and through each of them back to California — around the world in the space of a prayer!

Then north and south, and up into the sky, to the planets, the stars, to galaxy after galaxy, to the furthest edge of the universe, and finally back home again, here beneath the pine and redwood where I had left my body. This mind of mine, capable, as the ancient philosopher expressed it, of becoming all things, has become for the duration of 15 or 20 minutes the whole of the universe, and all of it better for my having journeyed through it. It is blessed now not just by God but by God in and through me.

In much the same way I can travel back in time — to my youth and childhood and all the history surrounding them; through century upon century to my most distant ancestors and all the history that fashioned and was fashioned by them; further still to the first rumblings of the nascent universe and that first light out of dark; all the way back even to when there was only God and the ineffable love that was to burst in the explosion of joy we call creation.

People, places, and events come to mind during this prayer that may be only of my imagining, but sometimes there's more to it than that — a seeing or feeling of what actually was and in some way, in *God's* way, still is. Shades of reincarnation! Only I need not believe I was there, but that it is here — here in my memory now one with God's eternal, timeless remembering. As in my simple prayer of remembrance sometimes a stranger emerges, shadowy and indistinct, yet demanding my prayerful attention, so now something real out of ages past flashes before me. I need not be disturbed by this or even surprised at it. After all, everything, whatever its place in past history, is present to God and so may also be present to me and now become one in my prayer with him. Remembering it, I need only pray it well and commend it to God's safe keeping.

This prayer of all creation helps mollify a nagging anxiety I share with many people. I'm sometimes troubled by the immensity and complexity of the universe. Its enormous size and detail is reflected in star and galaxy, molecule and atom. Time stretches infinitely, with the gradual, chaotic evolution of matter and spirit seemingly left to chance. And then there is humanity's long evolution and devolution—so many different lineages and only one eventually making it to *homo sapiens* and, after ages of unfathomable, incomprehensible history, to me. All this immensity and mystery, and to what purpose? In my prayer of all creation now and again glimmerings of an answer appear. Why not an infinitely vast universe when the God who made and makes it is infinitely more vast? Can so great a God make anything small? Even the atom as it issues from his hand must have its own kind of immensity, must be a universe in itself. Behind and within everything together, and everything singly, is this essential presence, this "mysterium tremendum" for whom nothing is small because he is great, and whose surpassing greatness is key to my own. For none of creation's perplexing infinitude makes any sense at all unless there's someone like me who is greater still, with a mind to match it, become it, to learn of the immensity of God in and through it, and pray it all, myself included, back to him.

9

SUFFERING AND THE DEPTH OF PRAYER

You say you can't pray. The Lord will
teach you in time.
Then maybe you'll wish he hadn't!

Prayer, we must remember, is not just a mental trip, a coming to know and experience God and our universe ever more deeply. It's not just a heart trip wherein one feels and expresses love for God and his creation. Prayer involves the totality of one's life: it must be rooted deep in body, mind, and spirit, and within God as he indwells in us.

"Hear, O Israel! The Lord our God is Lord
alone!
Therefore you shall love the Lord your God
with all your heart,
with all your soul,
with all your mind,
and with all your strength.

. . . You shall love your neighbor as yourself" (Mk 12:29-31).

Thus we cannot divorce prayer from morality, which is to say we cannot expect to pray quietly and purely if

our lives are agitated and askew. Prayer and life — they
form an organic whole, each issuing from and depending
upon the other. They are meant to grow together and be
of mutual help. If, then, my life is nervous and off-center,
let me pray, or at least try to pray, and little by little I'll
find myself living more calmly and nearer God. If my
prayer is distracted, arid and distasteful, let me examine
my life and change it till I begin to feel at home in prayer.

Because of this relationship between life and prayer,
like the tortured Job of the Old Testament, I seem to pray
most profoundly when I'm in deepest pain — when, that
is, my life is torn at its roots and all my old comforts and
supports have crumbled. "Out of the depths I have cried
unto you, O Lord," lamented the Psalmist in a song of
poignant truth. Yes, out of the depths. . . . I look back
now from this moment of relative calm and see how
deeply my crucifixions have dug into me, leaving me in
that emptiness and darkness I so value, dread, and strive
after in my contemplative prayer. I think especially of the
suffering I've experienced in the pain of others as I've
watched them lose all and die. Often, because of God's
seeming cruelty to me and those I've loved, I've wanted to
curse and be done with him. But so far my curses have all
turned to prayer, not overnight, certainly, but after days
or weeks or months of inner struggle. This prayer has
been most real to me and deepest within me, devoid of all
idols and self-centeredness, for the idols had been smashed
and little enough of myself remained. All that remained
was God, not sought now but thrust upon me with the
weight of his terrible, uncompromising love.

But more than my personal pain I'm concerned
about those who suffer much more than I have ever done.
My litany of those whom I've known personally is a long
one, and if I add to it all the broken children of the world

whom I experience daily through the media, I'm over-
whelmed by this vast sea of pain. It might not be so bad if
I could think that those suffering, though diminished in
other ways, were yet growing in closeness to the Lord. But
what is the evidence for this? Realistically, more than the
suffering seems to be required: One must somehow see
and accept God in and through it or in spite of it, become
prayerful within it. A holy preacher once said: "The pity
is not that there's so much pain in the world, but so much
waste of it." He did not mean to condone pain. He knew
that pain in itself is an ugly, destructive business. We
must, accordingly, fight against it with all the proper
weaponry at hand. Proper, I say, for fighting it in the
wrong way with the wrong tools, whether through added
violence or multiplication of soporific pleasures and comforts, only causes more pain on other deeper levels. No,
one must never become sentimental over suffering or un-
reflectively spiritual about it.

Pain came into the world through sin and is perpetu-
ated by sin. God is not its author and so is not to be used
in justification for it. He rather stands against it as against
sin itself and its every product. But what God in his genius and goodness has done is open pain up and make a
path through it to where he and his love stand waiting.
The path is prayer, and suffering transformed by prayer
becomes salutary and redemptive. So far that holy
preacher was right. We may add that it is in this context
alone that God may be considered a cause of pain,
namely that he requires us to make the hard and difficult
journey through suffering to him. He will not leave us in
the dark and terrible pit dug by the world and ourselves
but descends into the depths himself and all but forces us
to return with him up into the light. He would, if you
will, have us suffer the pain inevitable in the struggle

against the sin and pain caused by "world, flesh, and devil."

But what of the children, what of the innocent of whatever species who do not know enough to find the path or make the journey, who simply suffer and die in bewildered silence? What of those who do not know or refuse to know the God of compassion, perhaps for the very reason that their pain and the pain of others is so dark and terrible? I can suggest only one answer that does not entirely offend my sense of truth, namely that pain of itself is prayer, a superlative kind of prayer in which God is sought, loved, and found whatever one's conscious mind might know or not know, accept or refuse. The crucified, abandoned Christ draws all pain to himself and offers it in his great love to the Father so that both sin and pain might be overcome and transmuted into life and, eventually at last, into peace and joy.

I wonder if this isn't something of what St. Paul had in mind when he wrote of the prayer of the Spirit that's prayed within us:

> The Spirit too helps us in our weakness, for we do not know how to pray as we ought; but the Spirit himself makes intercession for us with groanings which cannot be expressed in speech. He who searches hearts knows what the Spirit means, for the Spirit intercedes for the saints as God himself wills (Rom 8:26-27).

Perhaps these groanings of the Spirit are our pain; and they are there especially, as St. Paul suggests, when we ourselves cannot pray. And might not this have been true of Christ himself? At the summit of his pain, of *all* pain, darkness covered the earth and he cried out: "My God, my God, why have you forsaken me?" (Mk 15:34). Was this his cry or that of pain itself? And was it Christ alone, or also the suffering he had become that whispered those final words: "Father, into your hands I commend my spirit" (Lk 23:46)? Impossible questions, I know, but worth the asking, if only to focus our attention more closely upon the relationship between prayer and suffering, and between suffering and the magical mercy of God.

10

PRAYER OF ACTION

There was always so much to be done. They
kept coming, hoards of them — hungry, alco-
holic, stoned, crippled in mind or body, most
of them stinking of cheap wine, urine, vomit.
And he'd be there for them, seeing they were
fed, cleaned, bedded, cheered, counseled as
needed, and loved in ways they could stand
and understand. Now and again in his busy
day he'd steal off to the little chapel out back
and try to spend some time with the Lord. It
used to be that he'd carefully distinguish between his prayer time, work time and play
time. But of late he began to feel the edges
blur and blend. Strangest of all he'd find
himself quietly, unexpectedly praying while
he worked. Little fits of abstraction, of peace
or pain, that took him not so much away
from his work as more deeply into it. He'd be
mildly shocked and embarrassed to find he
was actually seeing Christ in the beggar at
hand.

We often think of prayer and action as being at opposite poles. This appears to be most true when they are
most intense, for then each seems to leave little if any
room for the other. In our deep, consuming prayer of suffering, wherein we are emptied of all and rendered helpless before the world, our taste and strength for action
vanishes. Only God and his action abide.

Whereas when we are intensely involved in action it is we who are in command — dominating and shaping our environment, so there's scarcely time or occasion for thoughts about God. Thus St. Augustine's dictum: "Pray as though everything depended upon God, act as though everything depended upon yourself." Good thinking and sound advice, calculated to keep us balanced, appreciative of both God's and our part in the creation and re-creation of the world.

But the distinction pales as we look more closely. First, right action tends to beget prayer, just as intense prayer opens up into action. Whenever I pray deeply an energy and love gradually builds within me and urges me on to works of charity and justice. I may be debilitated for a time (and perhaps for a long time), helpless, unable to act, but only because God's wisdom, strength, and love are being formed in me toward more effective and creative action. Similarly, the more intensely and lovingly I'm actively involved with others, the deeper my prayer for them. "After you've changed the thousandth diaper," a devoted mother once told me, "you find you're helplessly in love with the little darling." Yes, right action begets love, love concern, and concern prayer.

Prayer itself, by itself, is action, possibly the most vibrant action we can be engaged in. Knowing and loving are inward activities proper to humankind, and prayer is knowing and loving on their deepest levels. It's this kind of action that raises us above every other creature and makes us most like to God, who is God not for what he does outside himself, but for his knowing and loving within. The prime and fullest act of God is the Trinity — the knowing and loving between Father, Son and Holy Spirit.

Action too can be prayer. "Whatever you do," says St. Paul, "do all for the glory of God" (1 Cor 10:31). We may

not in our action consciously reflect upon God but if in
our previous prayer we have emptied ourselves before him
and been filled with his love and power, then these will be
in our doing, making of it a sweet and pleasing sacrifice of
praise. Thus Jesus has told us that in our charity and justice toward others, independent of any conscious reflec-
tion upon his presence, we are nevertheless achieving him:

> "Lord, when did we see you hungry and feed
> you or see you thirsty and give you drink
> . . . ?"

> "I assure you, as often as you did it for one of
> my least brothers, you did it for me" (Mt
> 25:37-40).

Still, if we could maintain our consciousness of God,
our action might be even more richly prayerful. Just as
prayer at its highest pitch is contemplative — silent before
a God newly and freshly to be revealed—so our action, if
it is to be truly creative, must also be contemplative. This
not only means that we carry over into it images, ideas,
and feelings stirred within us in times of prayer. This, too,
but more. Our action itself should be such that it uncovers
God for us anew each time we act. Our every action
should be an act of discovery — discovery of God.

It's similar to a Bach or a Mozart composing music.
First, there's the original genius, that touch with the sub-
lime; then the time of emptying of old ideas, themes, and
melodies, of suffering and of loss; then the gradual or sudden awakening within of something new and different.
But the creative process is not yet over. As the composer fi-
nalizes in external sound the internal melodies and har-
monies, he or she is continually surprised by the new music unfolding to his or her touch. So in the larger realm of
living. There's the initial, fundamental oneness with God,
which is our gifted genius. Then the emptying, the forget-

ting, the suffering and the loss, which is our contemplative prayer climaxing in the dawning of a new realization
of God. Finally, in our acts of love and justice there is
God again and again, always fresh and new and full of
surprises.

Such action, of course, is rare. Always there's the
temptation, often succumbed to, to act first and then
think; to do and then pray with bated breath that what
we've done be right or made right.

There's so much to be done and so little time in
which to do it. There's so much injustice in the world
multiplying at a frantic pace. How, then, can we afford
the luxury to be still before we act and to be contemplatively still while we act? At least for now, let us consider:
First, unmeditated, precipitate action, however well-in-
tentioned and seemingly just, can only compound the
evils we seek to remedy. It makes us mere imitators of the
shallowness that produces and nourishes them, and lulls
us into thinking our pragmatic solutions are sufficient for
radical and chronic sickness. Secondly, what's needed
most is God in the world, not the mere word "God" or
our superficial notions about him, but the depth of God
and his revelation. For this, deep thought and prayer and
prayerful action are required. The world must be brought
to a new depth and height to allow it to achieve a new
perspective to see itself from above as well as from below.
How can this be accomplished by an action that is not
deeply rooted? The ancient adage applies: *You cannot
give what you yourself do not possess.* You cannot bring
God into the world by an action that does not itself hold
him. Finally, it's a matter of quality, not quantity — not
the number of acts you perform, but the kind and the ultimate effectiveness of your action. Like the poet who in a
few words and phrases reveals so much more than what is

actually said; like the God who in a single word spoken
out of the depths creates the whole of the universe and by
that same word sustains it.

As God's prayer is that deep and silent communion
between Father, Son, and Holy Spirit, which is one with
his dynamic action creative of the world, so must prayer
begin to be with us: We are to pray one continuous prayer
both in our solitude and in our loving acts in the midst of
our brothers and sisters —

> "that all may be one
> as you, Father, are in me and I in you . . .
> that their unity may be complete.
> So shall the world know that you sent me"
>   (Jn 17:21-23).

Injustice is found not only in individuals. It's alive
and active in institutions, making it difficult, sometimes
impossible for individuals to lead a decent and a moral
life. If the physical atmosphere in which I live and
breathe is poisonous and corruptive, my internal organs
suffer no matter how hard I try to protect and preserve
them. If I live within a society or under a government
that starves the body and corrodes the spirit, human po-
tential will be diminished. Some strong or favored ones
will survive and maybe thrive, but most of God's little
ones will grow old and die before their time, and not just
in body but perhaps in spirit as well.

If I am to be true to my calling as a follower of
Christ I must be prayerfully aware of institutions as well
as of individuals and prayerfully act to promote the good
in them and correct the evil. Further, my concern and my
reach must not be only for a specific society or nation, but
for the world, all of it. I have Jesus' final words on it:
"Go, therefore, and make disciples of all the nations" (Mt
28:19), and St. Paul's striking proclamation that Christ is

not just for Greek or Jew, male or female, slave or free —
not just for you or for me, but for the whole of humankind. As a Christian, then, I must be concerned about
numbers: My prayer and my prayerful action must reach
out to all.

As in my prayer of remembrance, here too I cannot
lose sight of the lone and lost individual, even if like the
Lord, I must leave the 99 in search of the one.

Today's busy world is almost exclusively preoccupied
with mass and number: mass production, mass media,
multi-national business, numbers of planes, ships, missiles
and satellites. Mysterious and massive economic, political,
historical and social forces overshadow and overrule, and
often bury the individual. My prayerful awareness and
action must begin and end with the individual no matter
where they may be directed in between. So like Teresa of
Calcutta, I must answer those who would leave the suffering individuals in order to address the injustice of institutions, with "One at a time." Each of God's little ones
needs, demands our love and care.

We must be large-minded and radical in our solutions to very large problems, and we must reach out to all
the world. But our prime concern must be with the beggar at our own door or within our own household, such as
mother, father, brother, sister, husband, wife, child,
friend or enemy. And realizing this may help us avoid the
panic and fanaticism of action.

My contemplative prayer, rooted in the divine,
teaches me that the time of ultimate accomplishment is in
God's hands. It may be tomorrow, it may be thousands of
years in the future. My job isn't to rush toward fulfillment
and be disappointed and bitter when it doesn't arrive, but
to act prayerfully now, especially with the individual, and
leave the rest to God and his servants of the future.

11

THE EUCHARIST: CHRIST'S PERFECT PRAYER

All I did that night was watch while he prayed. Three times I feigned sleep when he came and rebuked us. But what else could I do? His was such a perfect praying that all I could manage was to be silent, to watch and listen, and to wonder.

— cf. Mark 14:32-42

The most fundamental form of prayer is that of contemplation wherein I stand alone and empty, a beggar to my core, before the Lord of all. This is the prayer that gives depth and brings light to all others.

If after praying contemplatively I speak the Lord's Prayer or any other, the words will resonate in my heart: I will understand them and understand beyond them. If I should contemplatively read the scriptures or some other holy book, my meditations will be vital, revealing meanings needful for my life and love. If having forgotten all in the loving presence of the unknown God I begin now to remember, my memory will be bathed in grace and those I remember will share in that grace. The things I ask for will be the right things, and this unknown God will begin to reveal himself to me. If I come to the Eucharist with a quiet contemplative heart, it will not be mere ritualized word and act but what it truly is: the awesome, loving presence of my Lord and God.

Yes, contemplative prayer is the ground of every other prayer that would reach into the heart of God and raise us to him. But the greatest of prayers is the Eucharist. For the Eucharist is Christ's own prayer, his contemplative prayer which he offers in and through our own feeble yearnings after God. What the Eucharist, or Mass does, is make present for us those final precious days of the life of Our Lord, much too precious to have been confined to a single space and time of a now distant past. It is God's own "magic" by which he celebrates among us his one last supper and still suffers his crucifixion. So our Lord, at that closing feast of love, identified the bread and wine not just with himself, but with himself as sacrificed for us: "This is my body to be given for you. . . . This cup is the new covenant in my blood, which will be shed for you" (Lk 22:19-20).

St. Paul, clearly seeing that supper, the crucifixion, and the Eucharist as one, declares: "Every time, then, you eat this bread and drink this cup, you proclaim the death of the Lord until he comes" (1 Cor 11:26). He wishes to be taken quite literally in this and goes on to warn that "whoever eats the bread and drinks the cup of the Lord unworthily sins against the body and blood of the Lord."

Here is the reason why the Eucharist has been the central act of Christian worship from the earliest days of the church. It is a constant and tangible reminder that it is Jesus, the sacrificed God, who saves the world. Not statesmen or politicians, priests or prophets, artists or poets; not husband or wife or parents or children, however helpful they may be in the spheres of our lives. It is Jesus laying down his life for us as we experience him in and through the Eucharist.

And since the Eucharist is Christ's own perfect prayer on behalf of the world our task is simply to say amen, yes to it. Like Mary beneath the cross we are to be silent and contemplative before this great and awesome mystery, consenting with all we are to what Christ would work within us and our world. Not that we are not to speak. We are and we are to sing and maybe even dance. Here, after all, is our salvation, visible proof that we are loved by so magnificent a Lover.

Here is the one occasion left to us whereby all of us might gather together in peace and harmony if only for a few fleeting but promising moments. Here is the house of our one common Father made our house by the suffering, death, and resurrection of our one common Brother. He prays forgiveness for each of us so that we might be one "even as you, Father, and I are one." Cause aplenty to speak and sing out together our joy. But whatever we say or sing must begin and end in a silence that listens for the Incarnate Word whispering from the cross: "Forgive them; they do not know what they are doing. . . . There is your mother. . . . This day you will be with me in paradise. . . . Father, into your hands I commend my spirit."

Though there is abundant room for joy in the Eucharist, there's also a place for sorrow. We are saved by Jesus' crucifixion, so we take our joy and give our thanks. But it is a crucifixion, a terrible event. We should think of this at the table of the Lord. Sometimes we become too aesthetic in our approach to the Eucharist. We want the ceremonies to be tasteful and beautiful and to leave us comfortable and at peace. We are to give it the best we have and nothing short of that. But when, for whatever reason, it turns out otherwise, we might remember that the crucifixion itself was and is no beautiful matter. We might think of all the ugly pain being suffered throughout the world, and all of it concentrated here in this present suffering and death of Christ. The Eucharist is the torn, dying and dead body of Christ but, as St. Augustine reminds us, we are that body. We've reason to take joy in it for its promise of resurrection and new life, and cause to make it as beautiful as we can, but we must not forget that within it we mourn along with Christ's own desecrated body, the lacerated, dying and dead Body of the world.

The Eucharist, then, is contemplative prayer par excellence. Certainly it's the summit of Christ's contemplative prayer. Often in his ministry Christ would steal away from the crowds and even his disciples, and go off into the desert to be alone with his Father. We wonder about that solitary conversation between Father and Son. Once we were given a fleeting glimpse of it through three of his disciples who witnessed his prayer on Mount Tabor. It was as though the veil that separates this life from the eternal was drawn momentarily and divinity burst from Jesus and brightened the environment.

Once having spent a whole night in solitary prayer we're told that Jesus returned to his disciples in early morning walking upon the water, so light and buoyant had he become through such prolonged and profound prayer. But it was on the cross that Christ's prayer reached its deepest, when that emptying of himself, which began with his conception and birth, reached its term.

> Though he was in the form of God,
> he did not deem equality with God
> something to be grasped at.
> Rather, he emptied himself
> and took the form of a slave . . . obediently
>   accepting even death, death on a cross
> (Phil 2:6-8).

Here was the moment of total loss: "My God, my God, why have you forsaken me?" Here was the moment of complete surrender: "Father, into your hands I commend my spirit." And in that same moment Christ's resurrection and that of all the world began. What more can be expected of contemplative prayer? And all of it is present still in and through the Eucharist.

The Eucharist is meant to be the pinnacle of our contemplative prayer. It actually becomes so when we realize who the Eucharist is and what he is suffering and accomplishing and we say yes to both with all that we are. It is at the summit because in its ever old, ever new form of the Mass, it stands as the pattern of all our praying from its humble beginnings to contemplative perfection. So the Mass begins with a penitential rite in which we turn inward and acknowledge the idols, clutter and sin of our lives, and beg to be free of it. Next, in the liturgy of the word, we find hope that we will be free of our sin as we meditatively listen to the history of God's saving love. Now we can begin to turn outward and let ourselves go, confident that God will take us up and keep us in his care. Thus in the offertory we actually do surrender ourselves in and through the bread and wine, symbols of our self-offering to the Father.

At the consecration, that supreme moment of our eucharistic sacrifice, again with the bread and wine we are emptied of self and become the body and blood of Christ: "The life I live now is not my own; Christ is living in me" (Gal 2:20). All is forgotten now, all is surrendered. But all is also returned, cleansed and added to as we receive, in communion, the very life of the Son in virtue of which we too now can say *Abba* . . . Our Father . . . and mean it. All that now remains is a final thanksgiving for this new life out of an old death, and the bringing of this life into the world: "Go in peace to serve the Lord and one another . . . *Thanks be to God!*"

Such a beautiful, powerful rhythm: from what we are at our worst to what we are at our best; from the turning from self to God; from the emptying of ourselves of all that is ours to the fullness of God and all that is his; from our life and death in desolate isolation to the most intimate communion with the life, death and resurrection of Christ. It is understandable how medieval and thence modern drama arose out of the seedbed of the Eucharist; how so much of the great art and architecture has been inspired by and has surrounded it; how the best of music has been centered upon it.

But this, though great, is the least of it. The Eucharist goes deeper and beyond all this. It is life itself, the greatest life and death ever experienced. And its greatest inspiration has been to draw countless numbers of people into this life and death and resurrection, making them one with the deepest prayer of the God made man.

The Carthusians, that ancient order of contemplative Christian monks, have as their motto: "The world turns, the cross stands still." Here, in the Eucharist, we find this still center of the turning world. And our best work is to say yes to it, enter into it with all that we are, and so rise with Christ to an ever new and better life.

12

MARY AND THE CONTEMPLATIVE ROSARY

"Ask for a sign," the prophet demanded. But he wouldn't, so a sign was given anyway — the sign of the woman. Not any woman, but *this* one: the bless'd maid with child, the lowly proclaimer of the greatness of the Lord, the radiant madonna of the stable, the heart transfixed, the ponderer of the mystery of her child lost and found, the assured initiator of Jesus' public ministry, the silent watcher beneath the cross, the begetter of the church, the celestial woman of the Apocalypse, the gentle apparition in and out of time and space, making the great revelation alive here and now. *This* woman who embodies the Spirit, as her child embodies the eternal Son, proving the motherhood at the heart of the one we call Father. The sign was given, *is* given. But the reading of it aright, the following it out, is another matter.

Many different forms of prayer have evolved through the ages, both in the Eastern world and the West. Some have lasted for a relatively brief time, others for centuries and are still alive today. The Rosary is one such enduring prayer. Once I thought I had grown out of it, but for several years now I have been growing back into it. Once it was my daily, sometimes hourly prayer. I always carried my beads with me, and held them in my hand as I dropped off to sleep at night. But then the Rosary fell from fashion together with the woman honored by it, and many of my old beliefs were giving way to new ones. But perhaps this was a good thing. Having achieved distance from something, someone I loved, I've been able to return with a love that's new, fresh, mature.

I think of Mary herself, the one who centuries ago inspired this beautiful, simple prayer. She is the greatest of contemplatives. Like her Son and together with him she emptied herself completely. She conceived God not just in her mind and heart, not just in her womb, but in the totality of her person: "I am the servant of the Lord. Let it be done to me as you say" (Lk 1:38). Throughout Jesus' life she pondered his every word and action and even, as at the marriage feast at Cana, initiated them. She was so one with him as he suffered and died on the cross that the nails and spear that pierced him reached deep into her heart as well. And as he was born again, this time as the church, it was she who gave him birth and who continues to nurture him in and through the contemplative silence, suffering, and action of each of us. She is in wondrous fact Mother of God, Mother of the church, your Mother and mine.

And I think of this woman's special prayer — simple but profound like herself. She adopts a form of praying as old, perhaps, as humankind itself, and as young: the praying on beads. Something ancient and primitive in me responds to this. The very word *bead* derives from an old Anglo-Saxon word meaning "to ask, to pray, to beg."

There are Buddhist, Hindu, and Moslem prayer

beads, and in our time we've seen the appearance of "worry beads," a pale vestige of prayer for those who are anxious but who no longer believe or think they don't. A need for security? I think so. A reaching out for something, someone to hold onto, like a child clinging to its blanket. And deep within each of us is the primitive child grasping for security symbolized in many different things and ways — the bottle, the cigarette, one we love, or money in hand. The thing is to find the right symbol, or the least harmful. My rosary beads have always symbolized for me holding onto God and his Mother. I've got to hold onto something, someone. Why not her? She'll do me no harm, and a world of good. I crave for symbols of God in a world visibly sterile of the divine. One such symbol I've rediscovered in the Rosary.

This is only one facet of this particular way of praying. There are the prayers that are said — the *Our Father* and *Hail Mary* — two of the greatest prayers we have. One is given by the Lord himself, the other a combination of the angelic greeting to Mary and the church's response to the great gift we have in her. These prayers are so simple on the surface but, like Mary herself, so unfathomable beneath.

Recall Ernest Hemingway's *Old Man and the Sea* — that old and rugged fisherman promising so many *Our Fathers* if he might only land the big fish, and then settling on *Hail Marys* instead because they were shorter and easier. Yes, prayers for the simple and for what's simple and uncomplicated in all of us, the child at our heart. Yet, as we pray them over and over again, like a holy chant, we're lulled away from the cares and worries of the world into the Father and Mother who alone can bring us peace.

There are also the mysteries remembered in the Rosary: the life, death, and resurrection of Our Lord — the joys of Jesus and Mary, their pain and sorrow, and the light and deep happiness of their resurrection. The Rosary, then, stands as a gracious companion to the gospels. What we read or hear in them we can now, in the company of Mary, ponder and pray over and learn to see and experience with something of her depth.

Traditionally, certain specific events in the life of the Lord have become attached to the Rosary. In the Joyful Mysteries, for instance, we commemorate the annunciation, visitation, the birth of the Lord, the presentation, and the finding of the child Jesus in the temple. In the Sorrowful Mysteries, the agony in the garden, and the scourging, among others. But we need not limit ourselves to these. There are, as given, five decades concerned with the childhood of Christ, five with his passion and death, and five with the resurrection events. But what of Christ's public ministry? What about those great and saving acts between his childhood and passion: his baptism, his temptation in the desert, his prayer, his sermon on the mount, his healing ministry, his transfiguration? We should, perhaps, form a fourth set of mysteries commemorating them, which could follow those of his childhood and, as public mysteries, lead into those of the passion and resurrection. We should feel free to think broadly upon the life of Christ within the Rosary. Whatever the gospels speak of is proper matter for this our gospel prayer.

Here, however, appears the difficulty with the Rosary that many often voice. How do we meditate on the mysteries when the words we are saying frequently run in a different direction?

The answer is that as one becomes practiced in this remarkable prayer, a harmony builds between word and mystery, not so much in thought as in feeling. What is said is felt to be at one with what is meditated. I'm not sure that I myself am at this point. Indeed, I must confess that while praying the Rosary I don't much think about the mysteries or even about the words of those great prayers I repeat. Only now and again, when I "catch myself up," do I reflect on them. Rather, I find myself thinking about many other things, I have many "distractions," as in all my praying. But with the Rosary I feel it's all right. You might say, even, that it's become my distraction prayer, my free-and-easy prayer. Thoughts and images freely come and go. But beneath all the ebb and flow there is a softness, a gentleness, a quiet peace that unfolds, revealing to me the presence of the Woman.

It's difficult to say exactly what I mean by this, especially in this age when many fundamental distinctions between men and women are denied. It's almost as difficult as to say what I mean by God. When I think of Mary I think of the woman of the world—that woman of the Apocalypse "clothed with the sun, with the moon under her feet and on her head a crown of twelve stars" (Rv 12:1). I think of Mother Earth and of all the fertility goddesses in a thousand religions. I think of the Mother of the Church, Mary's title most recently emphasized by Vatican II — the one who conceives and begets God's people as she did Christ himself 20 centuries ago. And, of course, I think of her under her grandest title of all, Mother of God. I think too of the feminine dark of the Chinese *Yin* and the shadow *anima* of contemporary psychology.

But all of this is too much, too grand and subtle and distant for me, and I believe it is for her also. Mary is given to us not so much that we might think of her as someone great, but as one who, like ourselves, is little and lowly: "He has looked upon his servant in her lowliness" (Lk 1:48). She's there not to be magnified but to "magnify the Lord"; not so much that she might be seen, as to insure that God is seen and loved. Sure, she herself recognized, and apparently rejoiced, that henceforth all generations would call her blessed, but blessed precisely because she knew how to become as nothing before God and so be filled by him.

Perhaps here is a clue as to the meaning this woman has for me and to the kind of peace I experience within her prayer. Like many people I'm often afraid of things I see and, worse, of things I don't see. And I've been afraid of God. It's all part of that immensity and complexity of the universe that weighs heavy upon me, makes me feel at times insignificant, lost, and helpless. Yet in Mary, we find one minutely small and insignificant in her time, but noticed by God and loved by him so grandly that he becomes dependent upon her. He awaits her "Fiat" before being born into his world, and remains with and is subject to her when he'd rather be about his proper business. Later he begins his ministry at her request though he himself felt his time had not yet come.

Finally he entrusts his world to her care: "Woman, there is your son" (Jn 19:26). Such power and worth given into the fragile, gentle hands of littleness. She's the incarnation itself brought to its fantastic completion. God became a human fetus, a tiny baby, a growing boy, a vulnerable, insignificant Jewish rabbi at a time when Jews were most insignificant. Still he's God and as such darkness to our minds; and we fear the dark. It's only when we find him in the frail arms of his mother that we realize in truth that he too is littleness and so to be loved rather than feared. But even if we still should fear him, we cannot fear the woman who holds him, who is all and only human and our Mother as well as his. Pius XII had something of this in mind when he wrote in his encyclical on the queenship of Mary that "while justice and mercy be-

long to the King, mercy alone belongs to the Queen." It's
as though God in his immense understanding and mercy
wanted to insure that we'd always have a way out of our
fears and be able to realize our dignity and worth however small we may appear before him. When we would
fear him, the unknown, and even Jesus in his mystery, we
would not fear Mary in her utter simplicity and lowliness.

Is it this that makes me respond to Mary, to feel at
peace when I hold her beads and speak her name? She,
the very gentleness of God, his own littleness, his earthi-
ness, his maternal care for me — for me, so desperate always for the touch and embrace of this Woman beyond all
women. This is why Mary is so essential to Christianity
and to prayer. This is what the Rosary reveals within the
gospel. Not Mary the abstraction, the mere embodiment
or personification of my longings for the feminine, not
just the woman of the world or the Mother of the Church.
But the individual, tangible person who continually
brings God to me and me to God beyond fear and in love.
Not that God loses his immensity and mystery thereby
and I my awe and wonder in his presence. But that now,
thanks to my Mother and the prayer she teaches me, I see
God in the small as well as the great, with a joyous wonder and a happy awe.

6

THE STILL POINT: AN EPILOGUE

This is all, there is no more
Not yesterday or tomorrow
What I said or am about to say
Nothing I was or perhaps will be

It's all here, it's all now
Lifted skyward on soaring redwood
Lighted inward by dance of sun
On bark and leaf and dark damp earth
And there at the wood's tapered edge
The grey and wrinkled sea and all that cloudless sky

And here in this carved and windowed refuge
From the storms of other worlds
One and at peace with the tree that birthed it
All of it, all of it here and now

There is no yesterday, no tomorrow
Nothing done or to be done
Only the receiving like the Sacrament
Of what, Who, is — only the still peace
Of here   now   always